Urban Drift

Natalie Burdett

smith|doorstop

Published 1st February 2018 by
Smith|Doorstop Books
The Poetry Business
Campo House
54 Campo Lane
Sheffield S1 2EG

ISBN 978-1-910367-82-7

Designed and Typeset by Camilla Lovell Design
Printed by Biddles Books

Smith|Doorstop Books are a member of Inpress: www.inpressbooks.co.uk.
Distributed by NBN International, Airport Business Centre, 10 Thornbury Road, Plymouth, PL6 7PP

The Poetry Business gratefully acknowledges the support of Arts Council England.

Supported by
ARTS COUNCIL
ENGLAND

Contents

To my family and friends, and all the inspirational people and places.

Bridges

1. Hulme Bridge

Bridge-building requires work. Draw plans, consider risks
then take a first leap into air. Reach out and up from each side
eleven cables stretched to hold the steel parabola.

The arc looks effortless far off, ties insubstantial, delicate
but up close on the bridge itself you'll admire
foundations, span and mass.

Each cable thick as two clasped hands,
bound to concrete with a bolt of two feet by two feet;
each strut a repaid trust that goes on hoping into the future.

2. Trinity Bridge

A bridge needs care; commit to maintenance.
Protect the structure linking two proud cities;
each has its own shadows, so keep the bridge well-lit.

Tend to paintwork, watch for rust – thick moss grows out of soot.
Put down salt on frosty days. Be clear on boundaries,
who will cut the grass, who cannot be involved.

Provide for romance: late night walks across the river,
early mornings on the bridge's curves. Try to see from both sides
where you're going, even when it's dark.

3. Oxford Road Footbridge

Bridge-breaking isn't tidy. There'll be diversions;
inconvenienced passers-by will have opinions.
Feel dust caught in the throat. Concrete will stain

as cutting gear spills milk down surfaces. Break up hardware,
staunch wounds, see things previously held back.
Bind plastic sheets to scarred breeze block, chip board, plaster.

Wires will hang like weeds over blocked doors,
artery pipes cut at awkward angles. Hope in time for a clear view,
two smooth surfaces – detached, as if there never was a link.

Bobhowler

Crosses my room like a whip-flick then rolls, a grey Chinook
around the lamp. Too big for *moth*; its tremors take me back
thirty years to find my Grandad's word. I switch off the bulb,

but without glow it seeks heat, comes close slow-time,
low stealth-hum above my face. I slide under its buzz,
distract it with the landing light and shut the door quick.

Two words, distinct subtexts. That time we hung a sheet
on the back fence, used an outside lamp to call them to us,
we were unafraid – revelled in their glorious, mothy grace.

Toffee

Fidgety brick tries to be good,
stuffed in a greaseproof school-shirt,
collar tight and gold-stripe tie skew-whiff.

Remembers life in the pot –
a sweet dark hot mix – swirl and grit,
condensing naughty, spitting steam.

When crinkled bows are loosened,
rustled flat, it glistens to escape,
tries to run outside for morning break

but, trapped again inside a mouth,
acts up – its mass can't be contained –
obeys a lengthening instinct.

Can't go back – with each bite
ladders into smaller gobs of just itself:
a bright caramel laugh.

Boundaries

after R.S. Thomas

Where I'm from the boundaries are marked
by a DaySaver ticket. Chances are
your friends and family will be in the zone.

We value public space,
accepting that the benches are all steel,
covered in thick amenity-green paint.

We always ask, 'alright?'
not needing a reply. This is a grease
that lets us move so fast, packed in so close.

The market still sells shoes
and uniforms for going back to school,
but ASDA's cheaper now for buying clothes.

You have to move away
to not resent the sacrifices made.
Just don't expect you'll ever be content.

Smethwick Rolfe Street Station was always cold

I'm shocked by the fade in these remembered tiles –
self-portraits by five year olds from at least nine years ago.

I'd come round yours, evenings to watch 80s films
while your boyfriend tapped on video games upstairs,

then get a taxi back to Rolfe Street or, if we'd stayed sober,
drive past the glittering temple, my Metro aching with the chill.

I don't know how you kept your smoking from him,
or how you wouldn't shiver on the back step. It must be linked

to how at fourteen you'd fight anyone who dared
to criticise your fashion or pick on someone weaker,

and glide without a thought between the common rooms.
Later, you travelled the country to get back here,

where frost still highlights lichen splots,
but thickening soot on blue-brick resists time's blotched attack.

I'm still happy to train-it over – now you can't –
to share old stories and laugh at bad TV.

Berlin Talisman

Christine, the vintage plastic bird brooch
I bought at the market you took me to
in Mauerpark has flown away.

When I found it, delicate, without a tail
but singing brightly from a nest of tat,
I freed its wings, held it in my palm.

Afterwards, remember, we climbed high
above the music, drank cold beers, soaring
on laughter, watching planes take off.

Moving city, the bird came with me,
feathered my jacket as I met new friends;
after Christmas hugs-goodbye it had gone.

'Out of Darkness Cometh Light'

New platform signage has our crest and motto,
plus the added 'City Of';
Wolves station's now an *Interchange*.

The flour mills have been cleared
but at the yard back sheds still sag;
beams and willows poke through brown-tiled roofs.

Modern flats have better views,
but sex workers must feel exposed
unless they've been moved on.

Heading north, there's green
on the city edge, where the mist drops
and paths go where they always did.

The run of railway wires between their gantries splits the clouds, spreads, narrows, shifting limits, pulling parallels, loudhailer volumes broadening, slipping, fading to interference, forms a bubble of sky, a skip-rope, vogue dance, lasso curl, electric kiss, tension shimmer, interview, perfect cross of every possible diamond, framing fields, constricting chances, arcing to a gardener's stretch, momentum dwindling into dark, then coming back.

Arrival: the ring road tarmac shines
and the lock-gate paint's nail varnishy.
Hand prints are white on the bus-station glass.

A judge leaves court, loosens his collar,
blinks, as buddleia lolls in the old car park
and summer's last heat is squeezed out.

In front of the Bootmaker's building,
a rubble-field has been swept clean,
earmarked for *vibrant city centre living*.

The sun lifts all the ginger in a woman's hair
and new craft beer lounges are filling up
with early-finish workers on the razz.

The Soy Sauce Fish

Trapped, plastic body marked
not just with scales, fins, gills
but with a neat hook
at its capped mouth.

Doomed to be chucked
once empty – squeezed
for five seconds, crushed
and dropped to gutter-drift.

Lucky, it might float
bubble intact, spirit-level straight,
make its way back
to where the salt's external.

Why not re-fill the fish
with what you find delicious – let it live,
swim home, umami joyful,
sweet, salt, brackish, free.

Crow Flight (Oldbury)

The last commercial traffic on the Birmingham Mainline travelled in 1974, from Oldbury to Dudley Port, carrying chemical waste.

clear water   slow chug   coots rummage
lily leaves sucked balletic   undertow and wash
plastic bottles whirl   bouquet   thrown off in
grief / temper   greys   fades
bramble leaves   mouldering   dyed-black   dipped

in dirty water   move into shade   fat M5 legs
not safe   at night
tight turn   bad angle
fat silt slugs rise up   crawl from ooze-hole
thick suspension sickness   engage with this

buried murky water   run-off   spreads
between pale banks   escape concrete
to   open   air   tie up
upwelling bubbles   burst   surface sludge
brown + grey   tarry globs   rainbow slither

rancid water   soaks ropes   6 locks
400yds   yellow film   above top gates
stalactites   brick-drippings
lock-sides lichen-clear   gates 2 ½ tonne   ungreased
little-used   stiff   even at

level water   oil ghosts shimmer   split   coalesce
past unnavigable branch   former works
disturbed acids   phosphorus   cyanides
plastics   alkali   gas tar
ammoniacal liquors   sink behind us   towards Tat Bank

Negative Spaces

An old man shuffles past a heap of bricks
holding on one thin wrist a blue striped carrier,
eating a tray special mini-fish and chips.

Mortar foundation lines,
stretched out across tarmac,
chalk the corpse outline of a warehouse.

A weathered arch is crumbling;
grimy skin flakes off its bricks
exposing salmon-pink flesh.

A windowless former music hall
waits around for bulldozers, while dirt
in its guttering sustains a silver birch.

The underpass like a clean but empty fridge
steers us around the ziggurat –
peeled back to its spice-rack core.

A sky-blue fire exit ledge furs up,
collects litter, becoming more inviting
as new austerities and colder winds move in.

The Back Routes

Pale blue paint continues, thick with drips,
onto a damp course, where cracked cladding
fell to crumble on the pavement.

Salt leaches pale strings down brick walls
near piecemeal back-gate facelifts,
patched-up in the wrong skin tone.

Sunshine flickers through alleys,
between terraces, glorifying broken TVs,
bin bags, plastic bikes.

Gas escapes from a cut brass pipe,
like hot air brewing in the city
hour by hour.

A pepper-shake of starlings
over the markets. Home to roost,
shopped-out, spent-up.

Birmingham,

you're blossoming new curves. A warm glow skims
them, ribbons out across your city roofs
from Selfridges' bright aluminium discs,
to flick around the library's gold hoops.

At night a colder, more fluorescent sheen
accentuates your skyline's harder-edged
old towers. Polished steel casts well-built beams
of light which flash back from wet tarmac beds.

Inside the markets people claim a space.
Chermoula chicken couscous in deep bowls
steams up the glass; revives, illuminates
the dust-grey faces, highlights natural tones.

Outside, down low where nothing shines at all,
a sycamore seed sprouts against a wall.

New York

A photo of the Chrysler Building – up close,
fuzzy, canvas corner sun-scorched white.

Yellow taxis braid the avenues at dusk,
pass spirits gathering card in shopping trollies.

The reservoir is a black bear behind the joggers
and my shadow is clearer cut than I am.

On the Brooklyn Bridge, each tourist stall's
a measure of miles travelled, heart-beats hustled.

I hold tight to subway poles
as tunnel-lights run along the carriage floor like mice.

In Washington Square Park, a deli box in sunshine,
with wafts of agitation and jazz clarinet.

June Dusk

not half-light – full but indigo, shapes the world
like blue-screen magic, thickening outlines, messing with perspective –
distance melts, head-lights are ninja-fast

sodium orange streetlights flare against the blues all crowding-in,
cruel in opposition, expanding out doll-eyelashes /
haloes painted by Van Gogh, animate every leaf

plunged in a sea of sky I'm Jacques Cousteau – at jelly depths
and pressured fathoms on the spectrum edge,
in-lit with ultraviolet in the realms of bog-eyed fish

honeysuckle scent distilled to Class A-potency
by un-smudged skies magics a lapse,
while sun-burnt skin that can't trap heat feels doubly cool

Subjunctive

Homework: Compose a letter from Alberto,
living abroad, thinking of Paola.

Use this mood. In Spanish
it is required in many situations.

Perhaps, start with *I hope you're well.*
Try not to say *Wish you were here.*

Don't channel the obvious romantic
but a hopeful voice; careful

(but not English). For instance
I would like to see you,

or slightly bolder *It would be good*
if you came to visit. Then, directly

The truth is, Paola, I'm in love with you.
La verdad es, Paola, estoy enamorado de ti.

The letter should still sound like you.
Has it said almost what you hoped for?

Green Jack

When we first met I was all eyes,
small by his side, felled
by his deep shade and lack of need.

His lichen jumper was torn.
I traced thick oil-paint textures
of an old scar in his trunk.

His beard tickled my face –
his scent's more floral than you'd think.
His campaigns of silence

lasted weeks, eventually
wore me down.
I ached for conversation,

admired the brambles ranging extrovert
but feared their prickles.
Robins understood his solitude;

he tolerated them,
was careless about men.
He'll shelter you, but not in storms

and probably won't call
– too tied to his values.
I only went to see him once.

Tunnelling

racketing of air pushed up too-close against soot-suffocated walls as we squeeze through   friction scraping
brick-skin dry   clattering bones of windows   squalls wolf-whistling between us and the black   scream
of rails pinned tight and sinking under us   volatility of air crushed almost to condensing   sudden dash and gulp of exit
to a new and almost reassuring dark

Blood

One sleeve rolled back
I sit, wait, looking the other way,
for the prickle, click, outflow
while she asks if it's still raining – she's good,
but puts the vials in my sight-line and it's dark,
almost black. They'll be sent off,
just hold my breath for two more weeks.

We meet half way
for a picnic and riverside walk.
Now our parents are tired, ready for home,
so I'm dropped off at the station,
and I have to jump out quick – there's no space to park.
No hugs. I wave, grinning hard,
but hurting as they drive away.

The South Wales train
has passed by lost coasts,
declining towns and industry to reach here,
and the wide window opposite
is smeared with animal blood – a cow was frightened
onto the tracks. I've missed my connection
and don't know what time I'll get back.

Calder Storm-Brew

This is not my landscape:
all upright, vertical,
mill tower, moor-side.

Jets climb above
Walsden's top ridge,
where sheep mope,

and trees shiver
as September switches off
their chlorophyll

turning foliage
rust, blood, fox-fur,
mottled yellow week-old-bruise.

Millstone Grit is sootiest
high up, intensely black
on edges, corners.

Traffic hum blends with lark-song
and the flowing, sepia water
of the Rochdale Canal;

Klimt-gilded birch leaves
gather for safety
at the top end of the lock.

Bethesda

My questions tread carefully,
risky as the wet stone steps
but she's happy to talk.
The old hospital's stone walls,
broken by encroaching trees,
trap workers' ghosts,
hold their stories close and tangible.

Across the quarry's steep rim
mountain ash berries burn red against the lake –
dark blue despite the slate-grey sky.
The new zip-wire shrieks
but tourists swoop to its thrills,
put-on the orange overalls
– pure excavation-chic.

A squall flashes-back to danger
and I flinch, but she feels safe here,
closest to her 'taid'.
Slate piles settle, sharp edges
smoothed over decades.
Prevailing winds scour one side
of each heap's fine moss coat.

The Great Flood, 1872

Corpses rose from city centre graves.
Rescue parties salvaged stranded bones,
from the morass of headstones, bridge-parts,
bloated flesh and boundless mud.

Ladies hurrying past used pretty hankies,
so the council rushed to shift bodies outside the city walls.
Priests challenged the official estimates
of seventy six lost, and all restored.

The Medlock was channelled between terracotta bricks,
forced into hiding behind a rusty fence.
The city outgrew human dreams, on borrowed land;
the floodplain waited under concrete.

Baggeridge

1.

After heavy rain, water is trapped
near the surface by a layer of clay
red as a Staffordshire bull terrier,
collects in puddles of orangeade
then overflows them, streaming across fields,

cuts down through history
leaving tide-marks of black dust
on paths first cleared for coal trucks,
for open pits and deep mines
with seams that men could stand in.

Paths between Bag Pool,
Whites Wood and the Burning Field
have been re-laid with slag
to open up the territory
for walkers, foragers, birders.

Wash away leaf litter, to show young soil
then red gravel and white grit,
then sand and, under that,
knuckles of hard core, half-buried
in the clay that sticks us to our bedrock.

2.

Three hundred million years ago,
amphibians crawled out of swamps.
Giant trees staked their claim;
loaded with lignin, slow to rot,
accumulated where they fell
to form the peat that gave itself for coal.

Molten magma from deep volcanoes
charged through gaps in rocks,
hardened to basalt tough as Dudley miners;
eroded into soil and clay,
maintained a vigorous spirit,
yearning to find a way back into fire.

*

Lord Dudley gave away his granddaughter's hand
and bought back land with coal and limestone.
Three thousand men were employed to get at it,
send it up to Round Oak Steelworks.

A line of viscounts, earls and lords
sold the clay for high quality bricks, cut new canals;
created The Black Country. Left spoil heaps,
foggy ponds, budged earth, red water.

3.

Today an artificial spoil heap
dwarfs the brick work tower.
Below: two car parks, model railway,
café, orchard, wardens;
doll with half a leg missing
and soil-filled eye sockets;
an info board marked
by rust and cigarette burns.

With cleaner air, lichen is returning,
spread thick as butter along the older fence tops,
smeared on the edge of steps down to the ponds;
gathers itself in new blossomings:
a fringed bikini half way up a tree,
lavish furs on fallen branches;
seeping up the base of walls,
warming their feet as they crumble.

4

Sightings:

Great Spotted Woodpecker

Lesser Black Backed Gull

Great Crested Grebe Green Woodpecker

Red Admiral Small Tortoiseshell

Black Headed Gull Shoveler Duck Canada Goose Carrion Crow

Willow Warbler Meadow Pipit Painted Lady Dingy Skipper

Reed Bunting House Sparrow Reed Warbler Herring Gull

Pied Wagtail Green Veined White Long Tailed Tit Greylag Goose

Tufted Duck Sparrow hawk Holly Blue Mistle Thrush

Little Grebe Cormorant Marbled White Speckled Wood

Mute Swan Song Thrush Redwing White Throat

Small Heath Blackcap Jackdaw Redpoll

Chiffchaff Lapwing Brambling Brimstone

Siskin Raven Swallow Peacock

Swift Coot

Jay Wren

5.

The Miners Path is covered by a mat of fallen leaves,
and dead men's finger fungus gestures at the past.

In Whites Wood, black bluebell seeds prepare
and willow seeds make dark soil starry.

Down by Himley, sunlight stencils ash leaves
and a grebe pair chases peeping chicks.

The Burning Field's on fire with lavender-tinged teasels;
a flock of greenfinch swoop above them – well-fed, thriving.

Acknowledgements

Thank you to the following publications, in which earlier versions of poems first appeared: 'Birmingham' in *Avis*, Manchester Metropolitan University's creative writing student magazine, in 2015; 'Subjunctive' in *Under the Radar*, in 2016; 'Crow Flight (Oldbury)' in the Emma Press and Verve Poetry Competition anthology *This is Not Your Final Form*, in 2017; 'Boundaries' in the Offa's Press anthology *The Poetry of the Black Country*, in 2017. A version of 'Bridges' was shortlisted for The London Magazine Poetry Competition in 2016. A version of 'Blood' was shortlisted for the 2016 Bridport Prize Competition.

Thank you to all at The Poetry Business; Jean Sprackland, Carol Ann Duffy, Michael Symmons Roberts and all at the Manchester Writing School for their advice and support. Thanks also to everyone who has encouraged me, and all the poets who shared workshops.